EXTRAORDINARY WOMEN

Dilma
ROUSSEFF

Catherine Chambers

Raintree is an imprint of Capstone Global Library Limited, a company incorporated in England and Wales having its registered office at 7 Pilgrim Street, London, EC4V 6LB – Registered company number: 6695582

www.raintreepublishers.co.uk
myorders@raintreepublishers.co.uk

Text © Capstone Global Library Ltd. 2014
First published in hardback in 2014
The moral rights of the proprietor have been asserted.

Edited by Nick Hunter, James Benefield, and Abby Colich
Designed by Philippa Jenkins
Picture research by Ruth Blair
Production by Helen McCreath
Originated by Capstone Global Library Ltd.
Printed and bound in China

ISBN 978 1 406 27398 4
17 16 15 14 13
10 9 8 7 6 5 4 3 2 1

British Library Cataloguing in Publication Data
A full catalogue record for this book is available from the British Library.

Acknowledgements
We would like to thank the following for permission to reproduce photographs: Alamy p. 19 (© Rafa Happke / +55); Corbis pp. 6 (© Gregg Newton), 12 (© Bettmann), 14 (© CARLOS HUGO VACA/ Reuters), 22 (© HO/Reuters), 23 (© John Stanmeyer/VII), 27 (© Ricardo Azoury), 29 (© Jeremy Horner), 34 (© Noah Addis), 37 (© Anthony Asael/Art in All of Us), 38 (© Paulo Fridman); Getty Images pp. 4 (EVARISTO SA/AFP), 8 (Chris Mellor), 9 (CHRISTOPHE SIMON/AFP), 10 (Hulton Archive), 11 (Keystone), 18 (Gamma-Keystone), 20 (Mint Images - Frans Lanting), 21 (Jose Antonio Maciel), 24 (EVARISTO SA/AFP), 25 (SambaPhoto/Cassio Vasconcellos), 26 (NELSON ALMEIDA/ AFP), 28 (Eli K Hayasaka), 31 (DEA / A. DAGLI ORTI), 30 (Sasha Mordovets), 32 (Design Pics / The Irish Image Collection), pp. 35, 41 (AFP), 40 (CHRISTOPHE SIMON/AFP), 42 (DANIEL OCHOA DE OLZA/AFP), 43 (LatinContent); Shutterstock pp. 33 (© Rob Bouwman), 36 (1566-1033502), 39 (© Nestor Noci); Superstock pp. 7 (Marka), 13 (Ian Trower / Robert Harding Picture Library); Reuters p. 16 (© Ho New); Wikimedia Commons p. 17 (FrancisW).

Cover photograph of Dilma Rousseff, prior to the meeting of Mercosur in July 2012 in Brasilia, Brazil, reproduced with the permission of Getty Images (LatinContent).

Every effort has been made to contact copyright holders of material reproduced in this book. Any omissions will be rectified in subsequent printings if notice is given to the publisher.

CONTENTS

Some words are shown in bold, **like this**. You can find out what they mean by looking in the glossary.

Making history

It is 31 October 2010 in Brazil, and the votes in a tense election have just been counted. Have Brazilians chosen their first woman president? The city-dwellers of bustling Belo Horizonte prepare to celebrate. They are sure that their hometown **candidate** will triumph over her opponent, José Serra. As it becomes clear that Dilma Rousseff has indeed won, the deafening party begins!

Dilma Rousseff was **inaugurated**, or officially made president of Brazil, on 1 January 2011.

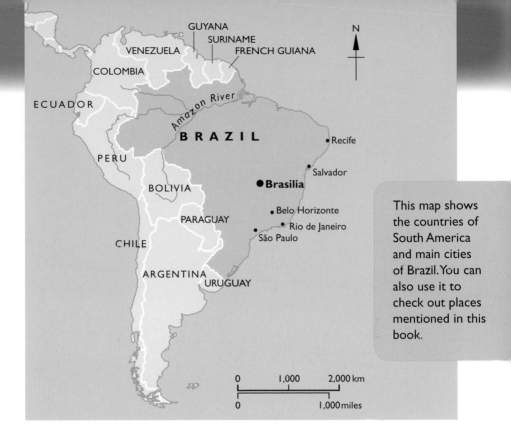

This map shows the countries of South America and main cities of Brazil. You can also use it to check out places mentioned in this book.

Dilma's celebrations were joyful but brief. She would be in charge of the world's fifth largest country in both size and population, with the sixth biggest **economy**. Dilma's Workers' Party had pledged economic progress for all, especially for the many poor among the country's nearly 201 million people. So how did Dilma Rousseff become one of the most powerful women alive? Has she made a difference? This is her story.

BREAKING BOUNDARIES

A FEMALE PRESIDENT

For the first time ever, a woman president stood in front of the victory rally in Brasilia, Brazil's capital city. The crowd fell silent. In a strong, unfaltering voice, Dilma made her promises to the nation. "We cannot rest while Brazilians are going hungry, while families are living in the streets, while poor children are abandoned to their own fates …".

Privileged beginnings

Dilma Vana Rousseff was born on 14 December 1947 into an **upper-middle class** family. Her family was educated, quite wealthy, and lived with modern comforts. Most other Brazilians were poor and did not have access to a full education.

Dilma's home was in Belo Horizonte, the capital of Minas Gerais state in southern Brazil. Minas Gerais is known for its mines and coffee growing. Here, Dilma's father, Pedro Rousseff, was a lawyer and businessman. Her mother, Dilma Jane da Silva, was a teacher.

Family is important to Dilma. Here, Dilma smiles at her grandson Gabriel during a parade. Holding Gabriel is Dilma's daughter Paula, Gabriel's mother. On the left is **Governor** of Brasilia, Agnelo Queiroz, and his wife.

This is capoeira, a martial art that includes sport, dance, and music. Capoeira is 400 years old and blends African and Native American forms, showing Brazil's cultural mix.

A blend of peoples

Dilma's mother was from a Brazilian cattle ranching family. Her father was from Bulgaria. His real name was Petar Rusev. Like many **immigrants**, he changed his name to fit with his new culture. Dilma has said Pedro was forced to leave Bulgaria in the 1920s as he opposed its military government.

Brazil is a mix of Native American peoples and waves of immigrants. These include Portuguese who invaded and **colonized** Brazil in the 1500s, and Africans shipped there by force as slaves soon after. Europeans from many countries came later, especially in the 19th and 20th centuries.

THEN and NOW

A man's world

As a child, Dilma dreamed of becoming a ballerina, a trapeze artist, or a firefighter, but never president of Brazil! Dilma witnessed the rise of women's political organizations in the 1950s, as they fought for better living and working conditions. But a woman president at that time would have shocked Brazilians and most of the rest of the world. In those days, almost all world leaders were men.

Dilma's childhood

Dilma enjoyed a happy, carefree childhood with her brother and sister in a privileged part of Belo Horizonte. Dilma's parents were interested in literature and the arts. This passion has influenced her greatly. Her father loved **opera** and Dilma has taken up this from him.

This grand opera house in Rio de Janeiro has put on famous performances since 1909.

Dilma also enjoyed cycling and climbing trees, and she was a keen reader. Her favourite books were about the fun antics of the comic characters that lived on Yellow Woodpecker Farm.

A dark day

Dilma's parents taught her that many Brazilians did not share their life of plenty. It really hit home when one day a very thin boy, dressed in rags, appeared at the front door. The very young Dilma had some money – a note. She decided to share it and gave a torn half to the boy, which of course he could not spend.

Dilma was too young to understand what she had done. But she carried the idea of sharing wealth into adulthood. She was determined to do something about Brazil's gap between the rich and the poor.

Dilma saw that women worked and had no doubt that she would, too. Teachers like her mother were great role models. Dilma knew, though, that most women could only work in jobs where there were few men. Could she rise above the barriers that women faced in the workplace? If so, education would be the key.

Dilma saw people living in poor parts of the city called **favelas**, like this one shown here in Rio de Janeiro. Newcomers build homes from whatever materials they can find.

Education for life

Dilma was educated first at Our Lady of Sion, a very traditional and privileged girls' school. Outside of school, she mixed with the **elite** of Belo Horizonte at the Minas Tennis Club.

But the school also wanted to teach its students about the realities of life for the majority of Brazilians. The girls were expected to climb the hill to Morro de Papagaio, a particularly poor favela. There, they worked as volunteers in the community.

Emile Zola (1840–1902) was a French novelist. He wrote *Germinal*, which showed poverty in industrial cities. Pedro Rousseff and his daughter were deeply influenced by books like these.

BREAKING BOUNDARIES

BECOMING AN ACTIVIST

It was Dilma's time at the Central State High School in 1964 and 1965 that really inspired her. Here, at just 16 years old, Dilma joined other students in Política Operária (POLOP). This was a new group of **political activists** belonging to the Brazilian **Socialist** Party (BSP). They wanted to free Brazil from **oppression** and poverty.

Dilma supported João Goulart, who was Brazil's left-wing president from 1961 to 1964. He was forcibly removed from his presidency by Brazil's military **dictatorship**.

While Dilma was at school, her world fell apart. In 1961, her father died. She was just 14. Pedro had encouraged his children to take an interest in **left-wing** politics, which supported the poor. Pedro introduced Dilma to some well-known left-wingers such as the Nobel Prize-winning poet Elisaveta Bagryana. Pedro had met her and many others in France in the 1930s.

Fact:
Dilma also learned about the struggle of poor people through her father's favourite books. Two of these were Emile Zola's *Germinal* or "Seed" and Fyodor Dostoevsky's *Crime and Punishment*.

11

Passion and protest

Brazil in the 1960s was not a free country. It was tightly controlled by a military dictatorship that ruled from 1964 to 1985. Brazilians could not vote freely for their government. Only two political parties were allowed, and these were carefully monitored. People who opposed the government were imprisoned, tortured, killed, or were never seen again.

At the same time, the government did not use its power to help the poorest people. Dilma wanted to see her country change for the better. Her passion for change grew and she was keen to meet more people who thought the same way. At university, she found them.

There was a military takeover in Brazil in 1964. The previous president, João Goulart, was overthrown by the Armed Forces supported by the United States on 1 April, 1964.

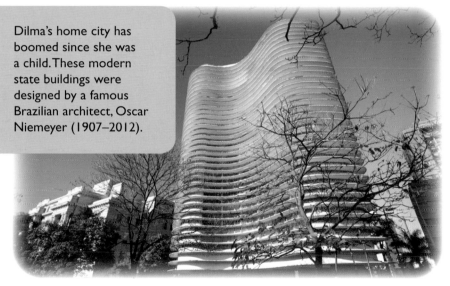

Dilma's home city has boomed since she was a child. These modern state buildings were designed by a famous Brazilian architect, Oscar Niemeyer (1907–2012).

How the world works

Dilma wanted to study economics. She wanted to learn how governments, banks, and businesses used and made money. She wanted to find out how medical care and education could be provided for workers and their families. So in 1965, Dilma gained a place at Minas Gerais Federal University Economics School. But she did not go to university just to study. She intended to join others in fighting against the military government.

13

Fighting for freedom

Dilma's activities in the BSP were not tough enough for her. So she joined Colina – the Command of National Liberation. This was an **armed wing** of the BSP. There, in 1968, she met and married Cláudio Galeno de Magalhães Linhares, who was a journalist. Soon, Colina changed into an even tougher group called VAR Palmares.

Some say VAR was a **guerrilla movement** – a secret underground army. Politically, it wanted the people of Brazil to own the country's wealth, from its mines to its factories and forests. This kind of ownership is part of a political system called **communism**.

The military government used **foreign investment** to develop industries like this oil refinery in Rio de Janeiro. This led some people to think the military were good for Brazil.

On the run

VAR organized workers' strikes, bombings, and bank raids. Its members carried weapons. Very soon, Dilma and Cláudio were on the run and were forced to part. Their relationship never recovered and they later divorced.

Dilma hid in Rio de Janeiro, where she met a VAR member who was a left-wing lawyer. His name was Carlos Franklin Paixão de Araújo. Dilma and Carlos fell in love and were married in 1973.

The "Brazilian miracle"

Between 1969 and 1974, world leaders and Brazil's wealthy classes praised the military government's economic policy, known as the "Brazilian miracle". Economists Amadeo and Camargo called it one of,

"the most dynamic and fastest growing economies in the world".

But in reality, companies and industry only made much of their profits by paying very low wages to unhappy and angry workers.

15

Turmoil and torture

In January 1970, Dilma was captured by military police. They discovered that she was carrying a weapon. The military court charged her with masterminding the robbery of $2.5 million from a safe belonging to a former governor of São Paulo, Adhemar de Barros. Dilma was accused of using the money to fund terrorist action against the government. She has always denied the charges.

This is Dilma, in a photo taken by the police in 1970. During this time, her secret name was Estela.

THEN and NOW

Brazil's prisons

Conditions in Brazil's prisons were appalling during the years of military dictatorship. But they're still overcrowded and violent. As president, Dilma has approved laws to improve prison conditions. In June 2012, she gave the go-ahead for prisoners to get an early release if they read or participate in serious study.

Dilma was tried and, despite her protests that she was innocent, she was found guilty. She had to spend two years in terrible conditions in São Paulo's **notorious** Tiradentes jail. Like other **political prisoners** and activists, she was brutally beaten and **endured** 22 days of torture. Torture was meant as a punishment. It was also a way of trying to force prisoners to reveal the names of other members of their organizations. Her husband, Carlos, was imprisoned, too. In 2012, Dilma said that her torturers dislocated her jaw. To this day, she has trouble eating. But Dilma also said that her torture wounds are part of her.

The grim gateway to Tiradentes prison remains. While the military was in charge of the country, countless Brazilians were imprisoned, tortured, murdered, exiled, or were never heard from again.

After prison

Dilma spent almost three years in prison. She got out in 1973. She rested her body and her mind at the family home and moved to Porto Alegre. There she waited for Carlos to come out of prison, too. Dilma left the armed struggle but gives no clues for her reasons. At that time, though, political activists and workers were gaining support against the military from the outside world, without having to use violence.

When Dilma got out of prison, the government was still strict. In 1974, however, Ernesto Geisel became president, and he relaxed foreign policy and also state censorship.

Dilma wanted to continue her studies but Minas Gerais University turned her away. They banned anyone who had been a member of left-wing organizations. But Dilma was accepted at the Federal University of Rio Grande do Sul, where she got a degree in economics. By 1975, she was working for the Foundation of Economic Statistics (FEE). In 1976, to her great joy, Dilma gave birth to a daughter, Paula Rousseff Araújo.

Dilma got her degree at the Federal University of Rio Grande do Sul, shown here. It opened in 1934.

Of her time?

Dilma now shrugs off her time as a more radical freedom fighter, saying she was just,

"typical of the 1968 generation".

19

Climbing the ladder

In the 1980s, Dilma worked for city and state government departments. She became Finance Secretary for Porto Alegre in 1986, helping to develop the city's economic policies. Then, from 1990 to 1993, Dilma served as President of the FEE, where she had started her career in the 1970s.

Dilma's star was rising. In 1993, she was appointed Secretary of Energy and Communication of the state of Rio Grande do Sul. Although still not **democratically elected** by the people, she said she wanted to serve, not rule.

Over 50 per cent of Brazil's energy comes from dammed water that creates **hydroelectric power (HEP)**. Half of all Brazil's HEP is generated low on the Amazon flood plain.

Electricity for pumping water is vital in remote rural areas. Using simple but effective technology, this waterwheel is powered by a stream of water. This helps to power a pump.

THEN and NOW

Making progress

In the 1980s and 1990s, Brazil's economy grew very slowly. It was made worse by heavy **taxes** on delivering energy, such as gas and electricity. By 2001, Dilma reduced the taxes so that Rio Grande do Sul became one of the few states where electricity was cheap and available to many people.

Dilma was faced with an energy problem in Rio Grande do Sul. There were constant power cuts. However, it was the same all over Brazil. Dilma warned the Brazilian government about rationing power, and she increased provision in her state. Partly because of this, people began to notice Dilma.

The election of Lula

Dilma delivered clear, surprising, fresh, and successful state policies. In 2000, Dilma left the Democratic **Labour** Party (PDT) and joined the Workers' Party (PT). It was the party led by Lula da Silva, whom Dilma greatly admired for his policies to help the poor.

Dilma campaigned four times for Lula in presidential elections (although sometimes for others in earlier rounds of elections). Finally, in 2002, Lula was elected as Brazil's first PT president. Lula was charismatic, and guided Brazil to an economic boom. Dilma had been one of his key assets.

President Lula celebrates with "pre-salt" workers by an oil rig. The oil lies below 2,000m (6,562ft) of sea, then 2,000m of rock, and finally 2,000m of salt.

This chaotic wiring in a Rio favela shows the need for a proper electricity supply in parts of Brazil. Dilma was determined to help provide it.

Dilma is recognized

In 2003, many Brazilians were surprised when Lula chose Dilma as his **Minister** for Energy. There were very few women in important **unelected** government posts and they made up less than 10 per cent in elected positions. But Lula knew that Dilma had lots of experience in delivering energy policies. Dilma knew energy was important for a nation's growth. She brushed aside any criticism and just got on with the job.

BREAKING BOUNDARIES

MAKING A DIFFERENCE

Dilma could now launch the popular Luz Para Todos, or "Electricity for All". She also helped Lula realize his Pre-Sal, or "pre-salt" project, which involved drilling for oil deep below the salt layers under Brazil's waters. Brazil's oil needs are now secured for many years to come. In 2012, Brazil also sold over 800,000 barrels of oil a day to other countries. But campaigners for a cleaner environment did not approve!

One step closer

The most important position in Brazil's government is, of course, the president. The second is the **chief of staff.** In 2005, a corruption scandal hit the office of the chief of staff, José Dirceu. He resigned. Someone needed to take his place.

Chief of Staff Dilma chairs a meeting of the United States and Brazil Forum, with the US Director of the National Economic Council in 2007.

A passion for helping others

Dilma declared,

> "A position in politics is worth nothing unless it changes the lives of the people".

A president had never before chosen a woman as the chief of staff. But Lula was no ordinary president. In the face of considerable criticism, he appointed Dilma. In Dilma, Lula saw someone who had already delivered. Someone committed to serving the people. And someone loyal to him.

A challenging role

The position of chief of staff is very challenging. Dilma had to coordinate all government activities. She had to make policies happen and be able to explain how, why, and when they would happen. She had to make sure that policies passed by the government were legal. She had to smooth over disagreements between the federal government, state governments, political parties, and others.

As chief of staff, Dilma supported the development of medium-sized cities as well as large ones. This is the medium-sized city of Araraquara in São Paulo state.

So how did Dilma do?

Dilma coordinated one of the most important government programmes ever. This was PAC, the "Growth Acceleration" programme, and it was Lula's flagship policy. It aimed to make life better for workers in city outskirts and medium-sized cities. It aimed to develop the whole economy, too. Quite a task!

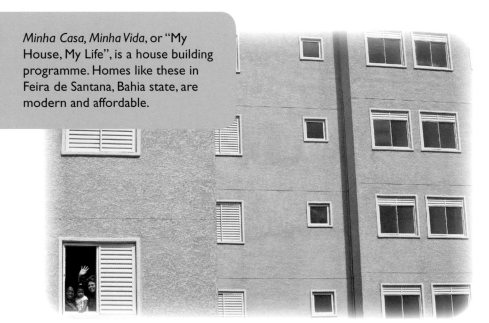

Minha Casa, Minha Vida, or "My House, My Life", is a house building programme. Homes like these in Feira de Santana, Bahia state, are modern and affordable.

THEN and NOW

A better life for many

When Dilma was growing up in the 1950s and 1960s, Brazil's economy did expand. But investors, business owners, and the middle classes employed in top jobs benefited most. Lula and Dilma aimed to help people out of poverty and raise their incomes and education to middle-class levels. They helped to improve the lives of millions of Brazilians.

While she was chief of staff, Dilma championed technology, aiming for broadband internet in all public schools, and digital TV across the nation.

PAC is now in its third phase. Under Lula and Dilma, it attracted business and foreign investment into Brazil. The government used the money for massive energy, technology, road, and house-building programmes. For Brazil, better communications, power supplies, and well-housed local workforces gave the poor greater chances. These also boosted business and industry.

A blow to her progress?

At the height of Dilma's rise in 2009, she was diagnosed with cancer. The illness affected the lymph nodes, which are tiny organs that help the body fight disease. Once more, Dilma showed her courage and continued working throughout her gruelling treatment. She beat the cancer, but would Dilma's illness stop her progress in politics?

Fact:
Dilma said little publicly about her illness. She allowed doctors to say that her cancer had been "resolved" and that her health was again "at normal levels".

Time at the top

In 2010, Brazil needed a new president. Lula had served two **terms**, each of four years. Under Brazilian law, he was not allowed to serve a third term in a row. So who would represent the Workers' Party in the election?

One of the candidates for the role of president was José Serra. He had been mayor of São Paulo. This city is pictured below.

A lot of people in parts of the Bahia region of north-east Brazil voted for Dilma. She appealed to many different people.

Dilma's name came up. But the press in particular had doubts about her. Did she have enough support? Was she strong enough after her illness? But Lula supported in every way the woman he called the "mother of the PAC", his government's flagship project to help the poor.

Dilma's opposition was daunting. José Serra of the Social Democrat Party was popular and charismatic. He had been a minister of health and governor and mayor of São Paulo city. Also, Marina da Silva of the Green Party was fiercely opposed to Dilma's energy policies, especially the use of oil as a fuel – oil can harm the environment.

The election results disappointed Dilma. Neither Dilma nor her closest rival in the results, José Serra, had gained the 50 per cent of votes needed for an outright win. Another voting stage took place and, soon after, there was a victor.

29

President Dilma Rousseff

On 31 October 2010, Brazilians showed their faith in this deep-thinking, hard-working woman by electing Dilma Rousseff. They believed in her passion and her commitment.

Dilma was officially inaugurated as president of Brazil on 1 January 2011. Her first task was to pull together the 10 smaller parties that had supported her larger Workers' Party. She soon got them working with each other.

Dilma began her presidency on 1 January 2011. She started by forcing 37 ministers to resign because of their corruption.

Fact:
During the election, Dilma was stopped at an airport by a young girl, Vitoria, who asked, "Can a woman be a president?" Dilma smiled and said firmly, "Yes she can!"

THEN and NOW

Queen Maria

Brazil's first woman leader was unelected. She was Queen Maria I (1734–1816) of Portugal, Brazil, and the Algarve. She was very powerful in Portugal until she became ill. Then in 1807, France, under Napoleon, threatened Portugal so Queen Maria sailed to Brazil. As queen she watched over her son, Prince João, as he set in place many rules of government that exist today.

Dilma's ministers quickly realized that she had high standards and expected them to work extremely hard. It is said that she has a quick temper and has made ministers cry when they have not prepared their tasks properly or on time!

BREAKING BOUNDARIES

"THE IRON LADIES"

Dilma has such a tough leadership style that she has been nicknamed "the Iron Lady". This name was given to Lady Margaret Thatcher, the UK's first and, so far, only woman prime minister. It is reported that Dilma dislikes the nickname as she disagrees with many of Thatcher's economic policies.

Dilma's aims

Dilma wants to create an educated, industrious, and wealthy nation. By 2012, however, the economy of Brazil had slowed down, as in many parts of the world.

Tourists can enjoy many stunning views over Rio. Tourism is being developed very quickly across the nation.

BREAKING BOUNDARIES

POLICIES IN ACTION

Dilma spends a lot of time meeting people to see if her policies have worked. She visited a farmer who once drove buses in Brasilia and asked, "How much do you make?" The farmer replied, "Four times what I used to make as a bus driver!" He is able to farm and sell his vegetables and chickens with the help of Dilma's electricity and irrigation programmes.

Goods are being handled at Vitoria harbour, Brazil. Dilma aims to increase Brazil's trade across the world.

The slow-down of the world's economy meant that a deep global **recession** had begun. There was very little money to **finance** development. However, Dilma managed to secure markets and investment from abroad, particularly from the **European Union (EU)** and also South America.

Dilma faced other problems, too. Labour costs were high and productivity low. This means that workers' wages were higher than the goods they made were selling for. People needed to work differently to produce more goods in less time. Dilma believes technology helps smart production.

Progress for all

In an interview with a British newspaper, the *Financial Times*, Dilma said,

> "We want this; we want a middle-class Brazil."

By this, she means a comfortable lifestyle for more people who will spend money, which creates employment and increases wealth. Some left-wing politicians believe that this policy could leave the poorest workers behind.

Challenges and changes

Dilma has spent her whole working life trying to find solutions to economic problems. But what about all the other issues that are important to people everywhere? Healthcare, education, and the environment are her other top concerns.

In 2012, the Action for a Caring Brazil (ABC) project targeted 2.7 million children up to the age of six. This took them out of poverty. The project will soon provide the same children with better early education opportunities and access to healthcare. Dilma sees this as the fruit of a strong economy.

Health clinics in Rio's favelas give children treatment and vaccines, and check on their healthcare needs.

Brazil has many modern hospitals, like this one in Volta Redonda city, in Rio de Janeiro state. But many hospitals in Brazil are overcrowded.

Good health

In 2012, plans called "Healthcare Closer to You" were made to pull together clinics in the **primary healthcare** service. These are clinics that include doctors' surgeries, dentists, vaccination clinics, family health centres, street clinics, and others. The service will also offer treatment for drug users as part of the government's strong anti-drugs campaign.

The government has also spent over £21 million on 24-hour accident and emergency departments in the huge city of Rio de Janeiro. There are plans to expand services throughout the country.

BREAKING BOUNDARIES

EXPANDING HEALTHCARE

A massive primary care study showed where services needed to be pulled together. In 2011, over 1,200 projects to construct primary care units were chosen through the "Brazil Without Misery" project. More than 25,520 units are to be built, expanded, or **renovated** by 2014.

Opportunities for all

Dilma believes that education, training, and research are vital for Brazil's economic future. She has said she wants to "create advanced and innovative technology, to raise our nation to join the most developed in the world".

Better education

Dilma and her education minister have provided for all, from toddlers to workers. Around 3,000 early-learning crèches will give toddlers a good start. In 2012, reading, writing, and mathematics at primary level were boosted through a testing programme that received over £195 million. Exams have been introduced at the end of secondary school, to test skills and knowledge.

Dilma supports training in traditional crafts. Here, a boatbuilder finishes off a fishing canoe in Camocim in the north-east of the country.

AIARA

36

Children are given meals as well as early learning lessons at a day care centre in João Pessoa, Paraiba state. Early schooling gives these children a better start in education.

Testing students has not been popular with some teachers but Dilma has not forgotten teachers either! They will receive 600,000 tablet computers and opportunities for further training.

Science students benefited in 2012 when 101,000 were given grants to study abroad under the "Science Without Frontiers" programme. The programme enables Brazil's students to share science knowledge in universities all over the world. Resources are being pumped into education projects for workers. They will enable working people, such as fishermen, to gain professional qualifications.

Top Marks

Barbara Bruns of the World Bank praised Brazil's education system:

"Brazil has one of the world's best systems for monitoring education results, and so it's ahead of a lot of other countries in being able to track how it is doing. It also has a lot of very dynamic state and municipal education systems".

What about the environment?

Dilma is determined to keep up economic growth. To help the economy, Brazil must keep supplying all its own energy needs. Dilma's policies have been criticized heavily by people who want to preserve the environment. Why?

Dilma supports drilling for new oil deposits, but burning **fossil fuels** contributes to **climate change**. Dilma supports growing plant crops which are made into **biofuels** such as sugarcane, which are used to run cars and machinery. But vast areas of biofuel crops are grown on land once covered in rainforest. Rainforests absorb carbon dioxide, a gas that contributes to global warming when released into the atmosphere. The rainforest is also home to rare plant and animal species. About 20 per cent of Brazil's Amazon rainforest has been lost through agriculture, **logging**, and mining.

With Dilma's support as chief of staff, laws on good waste management were finally passed after 20 years of haggling. Technology is Dilma's key to make recycling easier.

This wild giant anteater, or yurumi, is just one of hundreds of Brazil's creatures that conservationists wish to protect.

Dilma hoped to show her commitment to the environment through a new Forest Code. This sets out rules for clearing land and replanting trees. But not everyone is happy with it. Some are challenging the new code where it pardons those who illegally cleared forest before 2008. Some also oppose the right of private landowners to clear previously protected river banks and hillsides for farming.

Conflicting opinions

Jorge Ribeiro Mendes, the agriculture minister, declared that the Forest Code is:

> "...the code of those who believe it's possible to produce food and preserve the environment".

But Izabella Teixeira, Brazil's environment minister, said she was "saddened" by the final wording of the proposed Forest Code, which "lacks balance".

Looking to the future

Dilma Rousseff has received a mixed reaction to her position on the environment, but has been applauded for her work on the economy. World leaders have recognized the strides she has taken as leader of Brazil to help the poor.

Now, Dilma has the opportunity to make Brazil dazzle on the world's sporting stage. As host to the football World Cup in 2014 and the Olympics in 2016, Brazil could triumph – or falter. The world will judge Dilma on how she prepares for these global events.

Dilma supports Brazil's exciting sporting heritage. This "shark attack" move took place at 2012's World Championship of futevôlei, which is a combination of beach volleyball and football.

Fact:
Dilma likes to spread the hope and joy of Brazil's new sporting role. She celebrated the renovation of the Castelão stadium by kicking a ball between the goalposts during the inauguration of the stadium!

Dilma and her government are ploughing ahead with road, rail, and airport improvements. There will be new accommodation for millions of tourists. Twelve famous football stadiums are being renovated. The country and its people are anticipating a huge boost to Brazil's economy.

Dilma has gained respect for tackling all sorts of problems. Here she receives the United States' Woodrow Wilson Award for Public Service, 2011.

THEN and NOW

The right kind of preparations?

Brazil's government plans to move some of Rio's favelas to make way for the Olympics and the World Cup. There have been heavy crackdowns on crime in others, during which innocent people have suffered. In the 1970s, Brazil's military government also cleared the favelas. Is history being repeated?

What's next for Dilma Rousseff?

Dilma wants to continue developing the country she loves. But many questions linger. Will she get the chance? Will she be re-elected as president of Brazil in 2014? Will Lula da Silva want a comeback?

THEN and NOW

Still Dilma

So what remains of Dilma, the young girl who loved reading books, riding her bike, and climbing trees? She still has fun and enjoys being with her young grandson. Her love of reading and the opera has never faded.

Dilma has not lost her love of literature. Here she greets a Brazilian novelist, Paulo Coehlo, at the palace of King Juan Carlos and Queen Sofia of Spain.

Dilma's family is very important to her, too. Here she holds her grandson at his christening in Porto Allegre in 2010.

Dilma's approval rating rose in 2012 to 70 per cent of the voting population. In that year, many more people were able to find work, which has impressed the nation. Dilma has pleased many sections of Brazil's society. "By travelling less and showing greater concern about managing the country, she soon got the sympathy of the middle class, something that Lula took much longer to achieve," said Mauro Paulino, director of the Datafolha research institute.

Fact:
Dilma showed how much she cares after more than 230 young people died in a nightclub fire on 27 January 2013. Dilma wept as she said, "They were young. They had dreams."

But will Dilma Rousseff win another term as president? After seeing all that she has achieved and the challenges she has faced, what do you think?

BREAKING BOUNDARIES

OPENING DOORS TO WOMEN

Dilma has inspired women all over Brazil. She declared in her election speech, "I am not here to boast of my own life story but rather to praise the life of every Brazilian woman. I am here to open doors so that in the future many other women can also be president."

Glossary

armed wing section of a political party that uses weapons to force change

biofuel fuel that is processed from plants

candidate person who is put forward for a particular role or job

chief of staff important position in Brazil's government. The chief of staff coordinates all parts of government and all of its policies.

climate change change in the world's climate systems. Scientists think it is making the world hotter and causing more natural disasters.

colonize take over another land and rule it by force

communism system in which the main resources of a society, such as factories and farms, are owned and controlled by the state. Wealth is distributed according to people's needs.

democratically elected elected by people voting freely

dictatorship government, often unelected, that rules by force

economy state of a country in terms of production of goods, spending on goods, and the flow of money

endure suffer something difficult or unpleasant

elite richest, most powerful, best-educated people of a country

European Union (EU) union of many European countries that works to increase the wealth and well-being of all citizens, who can move freely from one country to another. Most EU members use the same currency: the euro.

favela poor area on the edge of a city or a larger town

finance support a business or other activity with money

foreign investment money from another country that supports a business or other activity. The money is usually borrowed.

fossil fuel petroleum, oil, coal, and natural gas. They are made from plants and animals that decayed millions of years ago and release carbon gases when they are burned.

governor leader of a local or state government

guerrilla movement hidden political group that fights with force to meet its goals

hydroelectric power (HEP) form of energy made by flowing water that turns turbines to generate electricity

immigrant person who leaves their country and moves to another country

inaugurated officially made leader in a ceremony

labour group of workers, or perhaps a workforce

left-wing political ideas and movements that support poor workers and those without work

logging cutting down trees to sell for timber or to make way for farming and other projects

minister politician who is responsible for a government department, such as energy, transport, or health

notorious famous for doing something bad

opera performance of a classical-style musical drama

political activist someone who carries out their political beliefs, usually by working for a political organization

political prisoner someone imprisoned for their political beliefs and activities

primary healthcare first place that a patient would go to for help with healthcare, such as a local doctor or childcare clinic

recession when the economy of a country or the world economy stops growing or even collapses. Recession brings job losses and also poverty.

renovate improve the condition of a building or buildings

socialist person who believes in left-wing ideas

taxes money paid to the government out of people's wages. Other taxes are added to the price of certain goods and services. Taxes pay for hospitals, schools, and other services.

term in politics, the number of years during which a political party governs a country before another election is held

unelected employed in a government position, not chosen in an election

upper-middle class people in a country who are well educated and live a wealthy, and comfortable life

Timeline

1947 Dilma Rousseff is born in Belo Horizonte, Brazil on 14 December.

1950s Dilma attends Our Lady of Sion School. She also finds out that many Brazilians live in poverty and is determined to do something about it.

1962 Dilma's father, Pedro Rousseff, dies.

1963 Dilma attends high school. She joins Política Operária, a group belonging to the Brazilian Socialist Party (BSP).

1964 Brazil is taken over by its military generals. Dilma is determined to fight for democracy.

1965 Dilma studies economics at Minas Gerais Federal University Economics School. She joins Colina, then VAR Palmera, both armed wings of the BSP. She meets and later marries Cláudio Galeno Linhares but the relationship does not last.

1968 Dilma's political activities force her to hide from the military police. She meets Carlos Araújo, whom she marries.

1970 Dilma is arrested. She is tried, imprisoned, and tortured. She spends nearly three years in prison.

1972 Dilma is released from prison near the end of the year.

1975 Dilma completes her degree in economics at Rio Grande do Sul University and starts working for the Foundation of Economic Statistics.

1976 Dilma gives birth to Paula Rousseff Araújo.

1970s–1980s Dilma and Carlos Araújo campaign against the military government through the Workers' Party and the Direct Action movement.

1985 Brazil's military government gives way to democracy. Elections are held to select a government and president.

1980s–1990s Dilma rises in government, becoming Rio Grande do Sul's secretary of state for energy and communications.

1994	Dilma's marriage to Carlos Araújo ends.
2002	Lula da Silva becomes the first Workers' Party president of Brazil. He chooses Dilma as his minister for energy. She is very successful.
2005	Lula chooses Dilma as his chief of staff, which is a very important position.
2010	Dilma is selected as the new Workers' Party candidate for the next presidential election. And she wins! Her daughter Paula gives birth to a son, Gabriel Rousseff Cavolo.
2010–2014	Dilma pushes Brazil's economy forward and prepares her country to host the 2014 World Cup and the 2016 Olympics.

Find out more

Books

Amazonia: Indigenous Tales from Brazil, Daniel Munduruku (Groundwood Books, 2013)

Brazil (Countries Around the World), Marion Morrison (Raintree, 2012)

Brazil and Rio de Janeiro (Developing World), Louise Spilsbury (Franklin Watts, 2013)

Brazil in Pictures (Visual Geography), Tom Streissguth (Lerner Books, 2013)

Website
www.brazil.org.uk/index.html
The Embassy of Brazil in London has a great website that guides you to events about Brazil. There are exhibitions and fun days on arts, crafts, foods, and more. Click "Events" on the Homepage column to the left. There are also other web pages with information on the environment, science and technology, and other topics.

Index